The Whale's Song

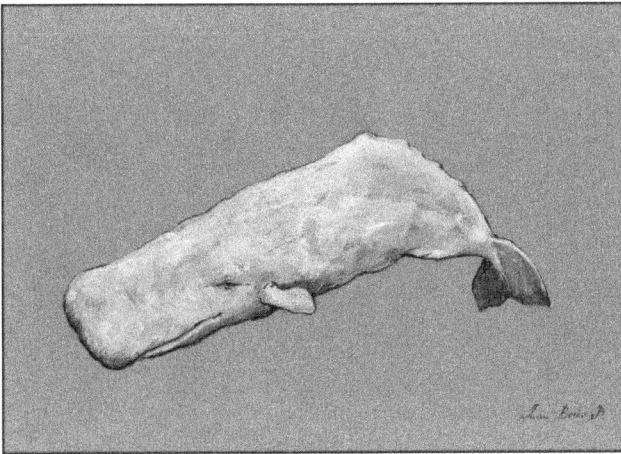

A Novella by

Casey Clabough

Finishing Line Press
Georgetown, Kentucky

The Whale's Song

Publisher: Leah Maines

Editor: Christen Kincaid

Cover Art: Juan Bosco

Author Photo: Anonymous

Cover Design: Elizabeth Maines McCleavy

Printed in the USA on acid-free paper.
Order online: www.finishinglinepress.com
also available on amazon.com

Author inquiries and mail orders:
Finishing Line Press
P. O. Box 1626
Georgetown, Kentucky 40324
U. S. A.

Table of Contents

We are not what we might be; what we are
Outlaws all extrapolation
Beyond the interval of now and here:
White whales are gone with the white ocean.
                    —Sylvia Plath

Ocean is more ancient than the mountains, and
freighted with the memories and the dreams of Time.
                    —H. P. Lovecraft

The Sea is everything.
                    —Jules Vernes

Many things I was called, though no true name e'er did I know.
I knew only that I was.

And that, in the end, was gift enough.

I. Beginnings

Back within the dimmest recesses of my head—so far as to seem the dream of another—lay the first thing: of treading the warm shallows in a hidden cove off the islands unlike any in the world. It was there I first felt Sun and my parts moving but slightly, holding me above the waters, between salt and light: wallowing in the midst of existence I would learn is called Life.

Yet with it, traveling to me through the waters, was Song: one I no longer may summon nor recall, except that it was a lament, a crying out. My eyes brought me the dim vision of a moving shadow far upon the horizon. My senses afforded me little more. But then I became aware of the waters around me, not as many things but as one, and a living thing it was—as powerful as life itself. And its name was the Sea.

I was not hungry; the Sea was with me. And yet something that had been there—that had comforted me like the waters—no longer was. I was alone. Had I drifted there or been placed there? And what of the strange brief song? Such memories were my first and in them lay questions such as these—to which no full answers ever would arrive.

II. Elements

It was around those islands I remained for a time. The Sea called them Land. Through her it had risen up, from a far place beyond even her deepest reaches. It had come by means of her brother, who was called Fire. The islands, then, chiefly were his creation, though she had shaped them as well. Together they had toiled to bring about what was. Yet even when Fire departed, returning to the deep place from whence he came, the Sea continued her work upon Land. This I saw and heard for myself when great black heaps of rock split off and fell into her with crashing, rumbling sounds: both above and below the waters. She knew I longed to know her brother and so informed me when next he came I would, but that it was not for me to go near him. *His ways*, she said, *were not as ours*. He cared only for his things, just as she cared for hers. It remained that for the things that were each other's, neither cared at all.

III. Necessities

It was in these earliest of times, when I knew so very little and relied so much upon the Sea, that I learned the necessary things. The light of my days was the work of Sun, who was father to both Fire and the Sea, and made possible all that moved both in the waters and on Land. The light of my nights was the gift of Moon, who was the Sea's sister. I sensed the three of them, as well as Fire, to be in league together in ways far beyond my knowing.

I learned Moon and Sun—but especially Moon—helped to move the waters of the Sea, while the Sea kept her sister close with the aid of Land. It was Sun, the father, who moved them all.

Moon and the Sea were close sisters, for as Moon moved so too did her sibling. When the Sea gifted her waters to one part of Land, she withdrew them elsewhere. And so Moon and the Sea were in league, as sisters should be, though not always in the same way. When Moon lay between Sun and the Sea, the waters rose highest upon Land, for that was a time when both father and sister helped the Sea to move. But then there were other occasions when Sun and Moon quarreled, each pulling in opposite directions and thereby undoing a little of the other's work. And though the Sea could not move so well at such times, she never took sides in their quarrel, but rather waited for it to abate. Though I had felt already her power, I learned then of her immense patience.

These were the necessary things and, for me, the Sea was the most necessary of all. Without her I never could be and never could have been. And when she knew of my understanding, she was pleased.

IV. Sustenance

I grew, feeding on Fish and, especially, Squid, who possessed a great many long parts. I sang as I searched for Squid, for my songs gave back where he dwelt. What did I sing of? Squid. For I knew he was there in part for me—a gift from the Sea—and so I felt that to sing of him was to give even as I took, which was the way of the Sea herself.

The larger of Squid was so strong in his parts that I felt their grip upon me even as I too squeezed with my mouth. His mouth, like mine, was hard though not of very great size. And while he could not sing, he could press with his small mouth as I did. Yet only Squid's mouth was hard. The rest of him was soft and readily filled my parts, even as I filled the waters with my song for him.

V. Remnants

It was the Sea who told me the islands were unlike any in the world and how they served as haven for her old and cherished things, which she called her Precious Remnants.

Among them was Crab, who took on new forms in and around each different island. Hard like Crab, but much larger was Tortoise. Like Crab he moved both on Land and across the waters. On one occasion, I grasped him as he floated atop the waves. Crushing his shell, I found him soft beneath, like Squid, though the taste was foul to me. Yet as soon as life had been squeezed from him, I knew the Sea was displeased. And so I made a song for Tortoise and vowed never to hinder him again. I knew then we had our different things to do—like the Sea and Moon and Sun and Fire—and that one never should seek total destruction of another.

I was learning what was meant for me and what was not, and so I let alone the other things about the islands—Bird, Snake, and Land Snake, who had parts by which to move—though I took note of all they did, and the different ways in which they passed between Land and the waters. From them I learned the subtleties of the simple. About me they moved like the Sea herself. And I watched them as she watched me.

VI. Whale

There arrived a day when through the waters came Song: a sound that was like and yet unlike my own. Then there were many songs, though none like mine. As they grew louder I took refuge in the caverns beneath the islands. Yet I also wished to know what sang. The Sea, sensing this, as she felt and knew all things, cast me in shadow so that I might wait among the outer caves to watch for what came.

When the singing grew so loud as to fill all the waters about me, I saw them: great dark shapes heading in all directions, but not without purpose, for in their moving and singing I knew they searched for Squid. I watched as they turned on their sides and then upside down, and in watching I felt in my parts how like my own movements were theirs. Yet as their songs were not exactly as mine, so their movements were not entirely the same.

That is when I knew the Sea had brought them for me. I felt her about me with all her great knowing, though in her vastness lay no expectation. She had drawn forth from the oceans those most like me, but left me to act as I wished. And because I was uncertain, she had hidden me. Yet I felt her watching, even as I watched those of—and yet not quite—my kind. And in her watching I felt her patience: a waiting far longer than life itself.

He is Whale, she said.

You are Whale, she said.

Yet of him there are many, she said, *and of you but one.*

And when Whale came closer, she drew me back into the caverns. I could not have joined them then, even had I wished it. Such was the Sea's care for her Precious Remnants when they were not yet able to care for themselves.

VII. Self

When Whale departed, I came forth from the caverns and surfaced. It was night, but such a night as when the Sea and her sister's light conspired, so that the waters bore Moon within them even as she remained high above. On such occasions it was as if Moon and the Sea were one and the same.

On that particular night I felt a peculiar urging so that I knew a thing was meant for me. I followed it, diving deep and, returning, rose high toward Moon, turning as I did so that I might look back upon the waters. In this way, Moon and the Sea gave me myself: a humped, glowing, curved thing. Larger I was, even then, than Whale and instead of appearing dark, I saw that I was white like Moon.

That is the part of me in you, said Moon.

The Sea remained silent, except to utter from a place far beneath the depths: *You.*

And so I glimpsed myself for the first time, observing that the thing I saw was unlike anything else my eyes had fallen upon and, knowing too, as the Sea had informed me, there existed no other thing like me in all the oceans—even among Whale.

Of him there are many, of you but one.

And so I leapt high from the waters a great many times, studying the parts I had felt but never before seen. And I knew Moon and the Sea were pleased.

You, said the Sea again, fainter, from a dark place within her deepest reaches.

You, she said.

For the first time I had seen myself and of a sudden I knew that in that one thing there dwelt a great many. Cracks, I discerned, between the ebb and flow.

Yet rather than answers, the host of new things took on the form of questions: Why did I share the color of Moon? Why was I with the Sea and not Moon or Sun? Why was I Me and not Other? Why did I begin and how? Why was I Only?

But then the Sea was about me and settled my troubled brow amid the waters. And all was silent save for a distant rumbling as when the Sea began to sing her own particular songs. Only this song was not hers, but that of another. Like hers it was and yet different. And, unlike the Sea's songs, which might take the form of Whirlpool or move high above the waters, darkening all, this singing arrived from deep below.

      Sleep now, she said.

      But what of the strange song?

      Sleep now, she said. *Brother is coming.*

VIII. Fire

Gently then I slumbered. For how long I knew not, only that within the depths of my rest there echoed the sounds of the depths below. And louder the song grew, even as I slept, until dream turned to waking and I beheld the changes wrought upon Land and the waters in anticipation of an arrival.

Stillness reigned everywhere and yet a stillness bearing hidden power. For of a sudden there burst forth an unmatched sound, as of all the songs of the Sea delivered at once. And then, from the topmost part of Land, there shone forth a light, many times greater than when Sun rises or sets, sending out his parts. It was then I first saw him—Fire—leaping upward from Land's highest point. Deep in color he was, as the parts of Sun on mornings when the Sea was sure to deliver a song come night, and his own song was the victorious roar of his deep rumblings freed at last.

Again and again he rose—not unlike those occasions when I sprang forth from the waters—only many times higher. And in my watching I discovered Fire was not brother to Land as Moon was to the Sea, for Land appeared to protest his arrival, filling the air with a darkness that obscured Sun and made day as night. But Fire was not content with these things only. Instead, he began spreading his parts over Land, moving upon it like Snake in great numbers. Toward the Sea he journeyed, bent upon joining his sister. Yet when at last he did, they roared in unison so that both Land and the waters shook and began to quarrel. Never before had I witnessed the Sea do battle. Until then, I had known her only for her patience and the things she did which were for her to know and do. But in fighting her brother I saw her in yet another manner. Fire feasted upon her waters so that they vanished, yet the Sea—in her turn—enveloped his many parts as they moved upon her like Snake.

As I watched, understanding struck me and I knew then Fire and the Sea had to fight—that it was a thing they must do, like the quarrels between Moon and Sun. And just as the Sea did not come between her sister and father in their struggles, so Moon and Sun remained idle as Fire battled the Sea. For its part, though wounded by Fire, Land grew in size by virtue of the quarrel between brother and sister.

I was not left unaffected by the conflict, for about me the waters increased their warmth: a pleasurable sensation at first, but then growing in such intensity even I was forced away, following in the wake of long-departed Fish. The contest worked upon me in other ways too, for when I rose from the waters I found I was not strengthened in my parts, but rather oppressed by the darkness which came forth from the joining of Land, Fire, and the Sea. I recalled the Sea's warning that I should not go near Fire and so I was not surprised to have been driven away, though the manner in which it occurred was something of which I could not have dreamt.

My dreams, I had learned, like so many other things, were gifts from the Sea and as I turned to glimpse again the parts of Fire pouring into the waters and the terrible rumbling song of brother and sister at war, I knew this to be a thing I was meant to witness. It was a sign from the Sea that had required her brother's aid. And she spoke to me even as she continued the sibling song of battle, for it lay within her power to do many untold things at once.

See how brother works, she said. See how no thing is safe in the waters or on Land.

Yet in such a way, she said, all things began and eventually will find their end. You, brother, father, sister, even me.

You cannot end, I said and though I sensed my thought pleased her, I knew it was wrong even as I uttered it.

Go forward now, she said, *until your end.*

But I am one of the things you keep.

It is not within your nature to be kept, she said. And with this there came a thing unspoken.

We all must do what we are, she said, *until our ends.*

And then I was alone, except for the ongoing brother-sister song of battle.

The Sea was with me no longer. The thing she had left unspoken was called Sadness.

IX. Departure

Go back then I could not, even had I wished it, for one cannot discover new oceans unless one is willing to lose sight of their own shore. Yet the Sadness of the Sea was not something I would bear with me. It was not mine, but rather one of the things she spoke of that was not for me to know. For other such things she had names, and yet for me but names only—Fear, Loneliness, and a great many others. But in this she was not displeased, for I was merely what I was, just as she was what she was. Neither of us could know or do what was not for us to know or do.

Young I was still and, though the Sea had taught me much, ignorant I remained of the mysteries of all the oceans. I knew it lay within the power of the Sea simply to tell, but that she wished another thing. So within me rose an urge that contained no further longing for the islands of my youth. Knowing was my wish—to learn what befell—and for that I knew I must search: to sound the uttermost parts of all the oceans.

And though she had left me and I her, the Sea would remain the same through each new wonder, and that somewhere she would be pleased.

Boldly then I thrust forward, the Sea no longer with me.

Alone I moved upon the face of the waters.

X. Whale (II)

In the midst of my travels I heard, on several occasions, the Song of Whale: the singing of those not quite—and yet closest to—myself. I watched as they moved and gave utterance, jets of sparks in fountains of blue leaping. It was a spectacle I usually followed, for I wished to learn more of him, though never did I venture so close as to be glimpsed.

Most often Whale sang of Fish and Squid while filling his parts with each. Since I already possessed my own songs for these things, I had no use for his. But other songs I found of value, especially those uttered by the old for the benefit of the young. Through them I discovered Whale generally moved in small or great numbers, but that every collection contained a senior master Bull who acted as guide, philosopher, and friend—as well as husband and father—to all who journeyed with him. It was he who possessed the strongest, farthest-traveling voice, which often sang of those who had come before and also both of things long past and yet to come.

There dwelt too in the master's songs both the history of his own being and the songs of those departed: of mighty Bull who had lived long ago—moving with their herds or alone like me—and of hard-won victories over Squid of great size. Yet there were sad songs as well: of beautiful calves and wise elders perished and mourned. And, of most curious note, were the more recent songs of Float Whale: a mysterious, silent thing of enormous size which never dove, but rather moved ever atop the waters. Float Whale, it seemed, possessed few parts yet often traveled at considerable speed. His hide was hard like coral, and when he drew near Whale, he birthed small, single-toothed young which had little things moving atop them. These young bit so deep as to threaten the very life of Whale.

Despite the things he did, I hoped one day to see Float Whale for myself. Dominion over Whale he sought—dominion by death, in which he nearly always seemed to succeed—and so the songs concerning Float Whale were mournful almost without fail. And nearly every time a single herd sang out the names of their dead, the composition lengthened until all the waters were filled with Sadness.

XI. Herds

Quickly I learned the lesson that not to search was not to have, and so venturing ever closer to Whale by steady degrees, I discovered my sight was significantly greater than his. For though I could see him at a distance, he could not see me—despite my lunar hue. And so I began to take note of him beyond the stories in his songs.

Always there was the master Bull, not only the largest and fiercest of his herd, but also its wise leader and the keeper of songs. Yet unlike Sun or the Sea, his place of authority held no longevity. As with all the Sea's creatures, the young Bull of the herd grew, so that eventually one challenged for the place of master. Such battles were waged with teeth so that mouths became twisted and deep wounds reddened the waters. At their longest, such contests transpired over two appearances of Sun and one by Moon. Finally, however, the mightier would dive and drive the other beneath the waters, pushing and ramming him away from the herd. If the youngster enjoyed success, he became the new master while the elder was forever banished to wander the waters alone. But if the younger failed, then he was the one to depart and join another herd or perhaps form one of his own. And yet things were not always exactly thus, for in rare songs I learned of lone Bull who scorned such rituals and chose instead to depart their herds for the purpose of traveling all the oceans, mightily increasing himself both in strength and knowledge.

So it was that as with all her things, the Sea had determined for Whale the things he could and could not do, but made also allowance for exception. And in this I felt her powerful imprint: her unknowable mysteriousness and care. For though her magnificent entirety forever would remain beyond my knowing, I steadily came to understand her in new and various ways—and always a little more.

XII. Pairs

As I watched, at a distance, a great many herds of Whale moving in the midst of life, I discovered also those among them who moved in pairs: the strong attachment of one to another—a thing I had observed before among many kinds of Bird. In Whale, as with some Bird, this connection appeared so powerful as to be severed only by death. And yet, even following the demise of one, the other clung to remembrance and forever sang alone the songs that once had been shared. I noted, too, the days particular birds, a very few, returned and so looked back—hopping along my milky hump or standing silent, reflecting on something long past.

When in the act of struggle with other Whale or Squid, the one unaccosted—be it the larger or the smaller—came always to the aid of the other, even if the intervention meant abandoning a calf or carried with it the likelihood of death.

I knew it was not for me to experience such a connection. As the Sea had informed me: Of him there are many and of you but one.

Indeed, the closest thing to this pairing of Whale was my own particular connection to the Sea. Though she did not require my aid, I knew I would come if she did—even should it mean the end of me. For I recalled she had come for me when otherwise I would have perished. And though she no longer was with me, it remained there was nothing I would not do for her so long as I drew breath and moved upon the waters.

XIII. Encounter

The Sea had taught me that to venture not was to live not, and that to seek not was to deny one's own teaching. Thus, before me lay a necessary determination: to move among Whale or remain one who moved alone.

It was one of those misty night-morns on which the ocean scarcely may be distinguished from the horizon, the clouds themselves drooping down into the gentle, grey swells so as to give themselves over to water.

Out of this watery meeting he rose, an old Bull, nearly as large as I and possessed of sharp eyes, which promised to reckon facts rare and short.

He had been watching for a time, for he hesitated not in swimming about me in circles, splashing his parts and disturbing the waters even as I rested upon them.

This, I knew, was the gathering: the assembly of power before its use. And I watched as both his speed and fury increased.

Then, suddenly, as he was just about to pass before me again, he shifted direction and propelled himself slightly above the waters, targeting my head.

He struck true and the force drove me back, though the blow he delivered seemed to cause him more discomfort than I.

When he came at me again, it was with his lower jaw hanging, as if he meant somehow to engulf me. Yet, discerning the true purpose, I let fall my own mouth. We arrived together—him moving, me floating—in a violent, mutual seizing of jaws, which he sought to twist by turning himself on his side.

Locked together as we were, I rolled with him so as to save our jaws from bending.

Furious at his inability to harm me in his grasp, he broke free and commenced again his circling and head pounding, though I felt the activity of the latter left him the worst for it.

Indeed, following one particularly resounding impact, the water about the attacker's head began to redden and he paused in the movement of his parts.

Slowly, then, he proceeded to move upon the waters—tentatively— as though gauging some new aspect of himself which had risen out of his own frailty, anger, and blood.

He waited as though he expected me, in my turn, to bring a new violence upon him.

This, however, I did not do. He had fought me, I knew, for his ocean, for his herd—for all he believed he was responsible for. I, on the other hand, knew of nothing for which to fight him and so had absorbed the onslaught while assembling no malice of my own.

As we eyed each other, bobbing amid the wave swells, his herd began to arrive and, before they caught sight of me, I dove deep toward a nearby coral field so that I might pass beneath them unseen. As I did so, the Bull sounded his song, which spoke of calm and safety in the wake of a mighty dispatch.

It troubled me not that he claimed the place of victor or that his herd knew not the shadow of some unseen power moving nigh below them.

I knew already this Bull's life would be difficult enough: that I had left him bloodied and stunned, and that he was condemned to endure the soft lashing of black waves until some other whale or circumstance, sooner or later, dispatched him at last.

Such was one of the saddest aspects of the Bull Whale's song, but also one of the most necessary. It made him what he was.

XIV. Float Whale

The encounter with Bull Whale increased in me the desire to learn of his dreaded cousin, Float Whale. If I possessed not the passions and habits of Whale, perhaps it was Float Whale with whom I would share a closer kinship. Yet, I remained dubious of this thought even as I entertained it, for I had heard the songs of the numerous deaths caused by Float Whale. And as I had no wish to harm Whale, I wondered why Float Whale seemed so bent upon his destruction.

The songs of I heard noted how Float Whale frequented the Ways of Whale, haunting his most populated ocean corridors which he used to feed and move about the world. And it was toward these heretofore avoided places I traveled, keeping away from Whale but remaining attentive for those who moved only atop the water.

When at last I encountered him, it was by sense of smell: an odd odor not unlike that of Fire at work upon Land. It came to me both in the waters and above them, a vaguely troubling thing that nonetheless seemed somehow familiar.

When soon after I spotted Float Whale, I marveled at what a strange thing he seemed: oblong, though his means of movement remained a mystery on account of the fact he possessed no parts other than peculiar, lengthy fins which rose out of his back, high above the waters.

His eyes must have been as far-seeing as mine, for onward he came, the strange scent announcing him all the more as he approached.

I had heard in Whale Song the strange notion of floating young, and as he approached—a hulking thing atop the waters with parts shooting upward—I discerned two of his youth birthed and come forth with curious little things—not unlike Crab or Bird—flitting here and there atop them.

I slowed to a smooth glide atop the waters, watching as they came.

First arrived one, then the other, coasting along either side of me, the little things upon them growing ever busier.

Indeed, so bent was I on the collective movement of the little things that I did not discern one of youngster's legendary teeth plunging toward my flank.

Squarely it struck, forcing me to plunge my head down beneath the surface and smote the waters violently in a convulsion I found involuntary.

Never before had I a felt such a sting, other than perhaps running headlong against rock or long-dead coral. Tiny it was in size, and yet deep and prominent.

Moreover, when I shot away with the purpose of escaping the discomfort, I found to my surprise the fang remained attached both to myself and the youngster, so that I drew them along even as I moved.

My flight brought me into the proximity of Float Whale and it was there I made a horrific discovery: the burning smell was not of Fire feasting upon Land, but rather upon Whale. Heat came with the sickening odor, and as it did so, there arose within me a cold notion.

Turning from the nauseating smell, I fixed my attention back on the sharp-toothed youngster and moved toward him.

As I drew close, I dove so that beneath the waters I pulled the youngling atop the waves.

When I surfaced I found the other youngster not far from me, and it was not long err he launched a fang, which splashed near rather than struck me.

Following this second attack I gathered myself with grim resolution, stretching my parts amid the rolling waves. Upon Float Whale's young I bent all my being.

I will bring my parts upon you, I sang. *Your young shall be left scattered and broken. What songs you have shall cease. And if you remain damaged, not dead, you yourself will make a sad living song to all you encounter.*

Toward them then I came, open-mouthed, raising the waves on all sides, and beating the waters before me into foam. I did not hesitate but moved ever faster, knowing now for myself that these younglings were but cruel murderers of that which the Sea freely gave.

Behind me, in my wake, there shone a path—a milky-way wake of creamy foam, all spangled with the golden gleamings of Sun—and yet it was a path no floating thing could follow.

Around them I moved in a circle thrashing the waters so that the little things grew agitated and no fang presented itself.

Then, feeling the time was right, I dashed one of them amid a large swell, so that it was tossed over on its back. One of its stray tiny things wildly sought to remove itself from my path, but instead I seized it between my jaws, and rearing high up with it, plunged headlong again, and went down. As I dove, I bit through the little thing and swallowed one of its tiny parts, despite the disgust I experienced at the taste of it. I let the thing go even as the waters reddened about us.

When I surfaced, I observed much frantic movement atop the remaining youngling, which also had collected the maimed little thing. Having rendered the youngster in no condition to give chase, I dove again and eluded the Float Whale in my course, until I vanished entirely.

XV. Belonging

The Sea had taught me the actions of things usually are the interpreters of their thoughts. So it was that my encounter with the Float Whale and its young showed we must be at odds. He had meant to kill me like any other Whale, but had failed. Did this mean I was aligned then with Whale?

Again I bent my mind upon the songs of Whale, listening as they echoed across the oceans. Day into day, night into night, they made record of things seen and heard. Among them even were rumors of me: a ghostly White Whale moving always alone. It was then I felt there could exist no speech nor language where such voices could not be heard. The songs spread out across all the earth, and their meanings to the end of the world.

Yet, for all this, I continued to feel it was not for me to dwell with Whale, since I knew that naught to venture was naught to have, and that there remained a great many things I wished to know.

On occasion, herds of Whale sang out for me in a chorus.

Come! Stay with us!

Be with us!

And yet these words were not truly for me, for I belonged to the Sea and no other, and so I remained silent, moving in my own ways.

XVI. Departure (II)

I had learned those who live with the Sea can hardly form a single thought of which she would not be part. And as I journeyed from ocean to ocean, I moved like day and night, but the songs of belonging haunted me even as I roamed. At times I would stop and listen to the tumult of far-off waters: The storm-dances of Bird, the barking game of Seal, both over and under the ocean. And ever ruling all languages and actions was the magical beauty of the Sea: weaving difficult destinies, allowing things to grow or die—making landed hills tower and mighty waves crash.

I knew each thing had its language and the things it must do, and though I knew myself as a resemblance of Whale, I treaded a different sphere as well, in which long ago there once moved things most like me.

Yet this only served to remind me how I was Remnant, Only, Last. And from that feeling I had made a song.

Forever wandering and returning.
The skies may lower, the Land may call it,
I know no resting nor yielding.
In nights of summer, in storms of winter,
Its surges murmur the self-same longing.

Oceanward I am ever yearning,
Wherefar is lifted its broad, cold forehead,
Thereon the world throws a deepest shadow,
ice-cold, changelessly melancholy,
It drowns the sorrow and drowns the solace.

No message comes thence, no cry is heard thence;
Its voice, its silence, can none interpret.
Yes, toward the ocean, far out toward ocean,
Where trails forever its own enigma.
By all forsaken, by Death even forgotten.

All the waters were silent when I sang the song, which meant even Whale paused to listen. And when my song was over, he sang in response from a great many places and directions.

Come with us! he sang, as I kept moving on, away from them all, even as I knew nothing in the world is ever truly single or alone.

Stay with us! he sang, fainter as I moved. And onward I went, until at last I could hear him no longer.

XVII. The Elder Songs

Though, like the wanderer,
The sun gone down,
Darkness be over me,
My rest a stone;
Yet in my dreams I'd be
Nearer, Nearer to Thee.

And it was through dream, the dream of that song, that the Sea touched me amid songs and wanderings grown aimless.

Drop deep, she said, in a sound that was dream, *like Sun or Stone.*

But where? I wondered in sleep.

Deep, she said, fainter, as if she herself were sinking. *Deep.*

And then there was nothing but the memory of her voice—a voice inside a dream—to compel me so that I began to dive as I never had before.

In the first days there was nothing: only the quiet of sand and darkness amid the ocean's bottomscape. But as I moved—as if guided invisibly—the waters changed as they are wont to do, the bottom growing deeper and rockier, even as my breath too grew deeper and stronger. Until at last, during one dive, I heard the thing the Sea had meant for me: a lost fragment of Song.

Warily I followed it—a sound like, and yet not like, Whale—until I heard it again, louder. Then I moved fast until the opening to a great cavern yawned before me. It was there from which the sound had emerged. And so I entered and found not one cavern, but many: what appeared to be a labyrinth of bottom rock. And from it, slow and irregular, emerged fragments of song.

It was a reservoir of sound I had discovered or rather been led to. Far below the waves, in rocky closed places, dwelt ancient songs that echoed endlessly, for most never found a way out—no open expanse in which to fully fade and perish.

I dove repeatedly, hardly marking day or night, for it was the elder songs I heard—those of my long lost kin—and I wished to learn and know them all.

In these labyrinthine caverns, places with but one opening, sound, so enclosed, continually reverberated. And in some of the deepest, remotest chambers the songs echoed near as loud as the times in which they were made. Such were the sacred Houses of Song and I would listen so long as I could stay, only to surface and return to them again and again.

These songs of old became my new teachers and from them I learned, so that when finally I sang in my true voice, within my songs dwelt the Elder Songs, like strange plankton consumed but destined never to leave. At last I sang myself and my own Song was as one of long ago. In silence Whale listened, for he had not the means to respond. And there was silence among Whale in all the waters except for my Song, for they knew who sang. To them my tale I taught. And when I had done so, I sang aloud long-forgotten songs of the elders. Yet even as I taught them understanding, a fuller understanding remained beyond, just as all the Sea knew remained beyond me. And though they listened long and close, none ever came to know that there dwelled across all my songs, knitted in part by the elder echoes, my one great Song: the Song that was the Soul of Me.

Even as I taught I learned one of the most vital of lessons: that one must reach the very bottom of things to discover that which is most precious and beautiful. And though she was not with me, I knew this as yet another gift from the Sea, so that my admiration for her grew larger still.

So precious was the Sea in my mind that all her various things could not be compared to she herself. After all, her waters marked the length of days upon sands the world over with their ebb and flow of endless motion. And so it was true the things one might desire could never be compared unto the one thing that was her.

XVIII. A Vision

The Elder Songs and the Sea had conspired to gift me a still larger idea of what I was. Name I had none and to Whale I was Remnant, Loner, Last. But the Sea had saw fit to guide me to those songs which otherwise would have remained beyond. And for this I owed her something beyond everything. I owed her myself. Precious she was so that all things assembled could not be compared to her. Her waters stretched over horizons far and dim, marking the length of days upon all the sands of the world over. So it remained that all the things that might be known or desired could not be compared to the one thing that was her. It was she who chose to answer many questions in just as many ways. Blue, green, grey, white, or black; smooth, ruffled, or mountainous—she wore just as many appearances. But this much was true: she was never silent. Always in her being dwelt voice and sound.

Yet these many things proved not enough for me. For I was no heaped bone collection of the deep, nor an ancient song echoing still. Air I drew, waters I parted, and my own song I sang. Yet where was I to go? What lay between moving and not? Where did time begin and end?

Violently, then, I parted the waters, avoiding still the others who resembled me in part— avoiding all things. All things, that is, except the Sea, who was no longer with me but whose gaze never left me—just as it watched over all her things. Possessed did I the largest mind of anything in water or on land, but it was she who knew all the things of consequence. Everything above and beneath her waters, she cared for—even a lone freakish thing such as myself, whose songs welled up from a time when even she was not so old. But in this I underestimated her, and not for the last time. The truth, in fact, was that her care for me was greater for that very reason, though I did not know it then—because I was last.

And suddenly her voice was with me.

Whence comes wisdom? she asked.

And when I answered not, she answered of herself. *Seeing it is hid from the eyes of most all living. But there have existed those who knew how Sun went down, the way thereof and the place thereof. To find it is to search to the ends of the earth—to weigh the waters my measure and know in their feeling what dwells there.*

I have looked, I said.

To look is not to know.

I look, I said.

It is time for you to see.

And of a sudden I was aware not only of the Sea, but Moon as well, and I knew something was meant for me. All about me was calm and above cloudless night, yet I felt both the lunar pull and the push of the waters, and how so little a thing I was in the grasp of Moon and the Sea. I was at their mercy and around me flowed their own unknown ways and secret sharing. I knew then these were sacred things Fire, and even Sun, failed to discern—despite all their heat and penetrating brightness.

So as Moon softly rose up and her sister swelled beneath, I knew I was meant to become aware of them in a new way.

Leap, they said.

And this I had done before, watching myself among Moon and her stars. Yet, unlike the first time I dove, Moon and stars remained with me—that is, I plunged into them and toward them. And when I surfaced again, it seemed not from the waters that I burst, but rather out of the darkness above itself. Again and again, I rose and dove, and each time I dove deeper it seemed that when I surfaced, I had come from a place deeper among the stars, where I learned there dwelt other collections of seas and lands. Even the pull of a great, dark Whirlpool I felt. Like the grasp of the Sea it was, only a thousand times beyond the size and strength of all the oceans.

Throughout the night I dove and jumped, and each time I arrived back from different places among the stars, which I learned were not the Moon's attendants but rather mighty suns rendered small by time and distance. Again and again I plunged and burst forth, noting all I saw, until at last my parts betrayed me. And though I could but barely move, the Sea bore me up and the moon shone upon me. Together they brought forth a gentle slumber and even as I succumbed, I knew it was for me they had done this thing.

XIX. A Shadow on the Mind

With the Sea I had mixed my body and soul, where the planet's center moves and the herded billows roll. Yet it remained this was not all and that a great many things remained. In fact, the very next day, stars passed over a lonely ocean, and I gleaned in their wake something more meant for me.

In the distance a dark Float Whale moved fast atop the waters. From it there emanated a curious familiarity as of a thing long parted and arrived again. And from it there issued a cold breath, not unlike the manner in which the waving sedges play with wind.

Failing to close with the Float Whale, I matched it from afar, but at last gave up the pursuit, blowing a single silvery jet as I did so. At this the dark Float Whale appeared to pause, as if it had glimpsed my eruption, but then on eventually it went leaving in its wake only that disquieting sense of familiarity.

Days, nights passed—some quickly as I watched the world about me; yet others as though each was its own eternity in which I might live out one existence among others. It was while gliding through these latter waters on such a serene night, many tides distant, when all the waves rolled by in a silvery silence, I glimpsed again the same dark Float Whale—this time at rest and apparently sleeping amid the light of Moon.

Fascinated, I drifted closer, yet not without a strange sense of revulsion. As I did so, I studied the thing. Decorated it was in a manner unlike any other Float Whale I had encountered. Sea-ivory adorned it, as did numerous rows of whalebone and teeth. An odd, fearsome thing it was: gaudy with its trophies and yet menacing nonetheless on account of its teeth and the accumulated bone of Whale.

I was not without my own pride and nearing its side saw fit to loose a silvery jet, which Moon chose to illuminate just as I released it. Amid the water and light it appeared celestial, like some plumed, glittering thing uprising from far deep waters.

Yet in the wake of the spectacle, the dark Float Whale began to stir, though by then I was far beneath him.

I took to following the Float Whale on account of his oddness and strange familiarity. And as I did, he grew upon me as a shadow on the mind—a dark, inexplicable thing occupying my thought.

Some days later, when I reckoned the Float Whale grown inattentive to its surroundings, I let go my jet during the same silent hour as before. And though the whale took note of it and tried to pursue, once more I disappeared as if I had never been. And from then on, I blew forth my solitary spout whenever it pleased me. And onward it seemed to guide and allure the strange Float Whale, so that he followed me rather than I him.

In this, a gentle pursuit compared to what followed, it dawned on me we lived and dreamed, not as we wished to, but only as we could.

And what followed were phantom days, granting no shadows of hope. Sometimes it was I who was the more ghostly. Other times it was he.

A vast silence reigned throughout the waters, as though the Sea had forsaken them. There was a desolation, lifeless, without movement, so lone and cold that the spirit of it was not even that of Sadness. Instead, it was mockery: the masterful and incommunicable wisdom of eternity beyond mocking the futility of life and its effort.

Somber lessons of the Sea returned to me amid my travels. Yet even as I summoned them, I recalled her cautionary urging: that to be proud of learning is the greatest ignorance and that all are equal in the presence of death. What guides us then? Accident, which is simply unforeseen order.

And with me also traveled the songs of Whale: singing of each other, of the happenings of life, even of me. What did they sing of me? A kind of consensus which had assembled itself across time. Among their songs was the firm belief I had come from the Sea of her own accord since they believed within my breast could be heard her roaring: her existence within the Elder Songs. They sang also of the pupils of my eyes in which lingered the mysterious and eternal horizon that the Sea rarely bestows as keepsake. And, lastly, they counted me alongside the Sea since the movements of my parts were sultry like the tidal breezes of full summer, fragrant with the smell of seaweed cast upon the shore.

Once, long ago, Whale had questioned me as to the nature of the Sea and how she seemed to care especially for me.

Sweetest the strain when in the song the singer has been lost, he observed, which meant he was no fool and so prompted me to respond.

What do the wild waves ask? I queried him in turn. *It is but the same, sad thing that is all of ours'.*

As for the Sea herself, I continued, *Hold her in your head, for to feel her is as a memory and to hear her is as a song.*

And then it was as if the thought of Whale had brought me into their midst. And not only him but the dark Float Whale too, who no longer followed but lay ahead. About him his young bit into Whale with their fangs and pools of Sadness drifted through the waters amid pools of blood.

Slowly then I moved into the tumult, looming up out of the water, looking to gain the dark Float Whale's gaze. And sure enough he birthed a new young, which promptly came on. Quickly I moved away, the youngling gaining swiftly—a fast thing indeed for having just been birthed.

Before he was fully alongside me the youngster's fang struck and the burning wound redoubled my movement atop the water, dragging him in wake. Then I rose and dove deep, taking him with me and leaving only a swift gleam of bubbling white water above.

Downward I plunged as if bound for the Houses of Song, toothed youngling my sole companion. Not until the darkest of depths did he relinquish his bite, though the tooth remained. And when he had done so, he moved not at all, save to drift and sink a little more.

Then I moved on in the darkness, vaguely knowing the Float Whale would be there when I surfaced.

Something had changed. The touch and go was over. Soon we would meet and match ourselves until things sunk down into night.

XX. The Attack (Day I)

Once, long ago, I had thought at length not only of what is granted and what is taken—like the moving dismembered parts of squid drifting into deepest dark. Rather, I had come to ponder how one might reckon one's inner time by tides or stars, days or dreams. Having tried them all, I was left wanting. Then, in dark, still waters I beheld of a sudden a marvel in the night. Not by the power of the eye, but rather the gaze that peers within. And as I looked, I felt awe in my discovery's simplicity: it was the heart alone that I recorded.

There is no such thing as accident; it is fate misnamed. So the next day I was not surprised when the dark Float Whale appeared behind me, moving quickly in his parts.

As he came, he seemed possessed of a speed the waters did not afford him, yet one that pushed nonetheless.

I studied him as he approached: not over large for a Float Whale— no longer than I. But just as my parts were not the same as those closest to me, so his parts were not as the others who moved atop the waters.

I had come to believe that everything I saw was the work of the elements, yet in him they had been set together in an order that was askew. As I have noted, his complexion was dark and from his wrinkled back rose spines which gave forth his fins. Lower, his neck was heavy with polished bone. Here and there I spotted the teeth of Whale. And yet for all his fierce parts, he seemed somehow afflicted by a Sadness unnamable—a hollow thing which lay muted behind his strange familiarity.

It was then, watching as he came on, taking in his form beneath the full warmth of Sun, that realization struck me: he had been searching, just as I had long searched, and the thing for which he searched was me!

For him I had been the star for which all evening waits. As for the Why no answer came, other than I was his answer. And yet in that I knew there lay both far past and far future at once, as when no thing had or will have shape: no thing to act upon another; no cold or heat, soft or hard, weight and weighted.

Then he was nearly upon me, birthing his fanged young, three of them, faster than I ever had seen a Float Whale give birth, and on they came, bent upon piercing me.

Turning away from them, I moved and thought, gentle waters about me, while upon my back danced the light parts of Bird in great numbers, alternate with their fitful flight. Hungry was this Float Whale and its youth for my flesh, but I resolved to have it wait while I moved on in quietude and thought.

Finding no course of action that seemed right amid my new knowledge, I dove suddenly, leaving them alone atop the waters.

For a long time I peered up at them from below before deciding, and when I rose I fixed upon the middle youngling, and spread wide my mouth. They had revealed enough of their purpose for me to know they meant me ill, yet they would feel my teeth first.

However the youngster above proved no fool when he turned suddenly, which forced me, in turn, to transplant myself, in an instant, shooting my head lengthwise beneath him and turning upon my back as I did so. Thus aligned, I slowly and feelingly took the flanks of the calf within my mouth, so that my long, narrow, lower jaw curled high upward. In this attitude, I shook the brittle youngster side to side, before bearing down with the force of my mouth, splitting him in twain and rendering him dead upon the waters, the little things making their faint songs and puny splashing as the broken parts of the calf that bore them drifted apart.

Then I swam about the carnage, thrashing the waters, and beneath them I sang my song. And as I did, all Whale Song near and far ceased. This I did until the dark Float Whale neared his broken young and I left him there in his grief, concluding my song.

It was then Whale broke his silence and struck up a song of me I had never before heard:

> *It is he! It is he!*
> *The lone one.*
> *The only one.*
> *The Last.*
>
> *It is he.*
> *The one who sings our fathers.*
> *Their songs in his, his song in ours.*
> *It is he who fights again.*
> *And sings the battle's song.*

Then their tale of me was taken up in untold numbers, until it filled all the oceans, and even Shark paused in pursuit of blood at the ringing of the chorus.

I had not breath for song so that I thought only, absently: When does the song die? When am I to be forgotten? My heart now harbors no counsel? How long shall this enemy loom upon each rise?

Upon the waters I moved in thought, yet, as if in answer to my last question, the dark Float Whale followed. I was the thing he sought and in that no question lay. Close behind he tread, for I tasked him still—I was his task—and never would he give me up.

XXI. The Attack (Day II)

For a time, there was nothing, I continued on. Kept on straight, I did. If it was me he sought to find, let him do so. Yet owing to his wrath or lust for my blood or whatever spurred the dark Float Whale on, it was a force that blinded and he would have hastened on past me had I not leapt in the water in clear sight, where even he could not miss me, so consumed were his eyes.

Slowly and smoothly he moved along the horizon's nearing line, until at last he birthed his fanged young, fast as before, and on they came, three more. But rather than let them give chase a while, as I had done before, I turned and came for them. And when I neared them, I worked all my parts in furious motion and rushed among them with open jaw, heedless of the teeth which bit at me on every side.

Strike me those fangs did and hold fast to the younglings, despite the tumult I made of the waters. And so I moved about and between them, rendering their biting an even greater challenge, and, what's more, making the teeth sunk in me their own enemy. For attached as they were to the younglings, they served to draw them toward me against their will. Dragged them then, I did, and though one set itself loose, the other two came on, the little things scurrying about them, until I moved so that they were dashed together the way a stormy ocean greets the rocks of land.

Leaving the two shattered, I dove, though not very deep, for I remembered the third calf who had come loose of his tooth. And so, turning in the depths, I shot myself up: buoyancy and all my moving parts inventing new speed. With such force behind my forehead, I struck the youngling from beneath so that he flew up into the air, not unlike a playful, benevolent young one making his first spectacular dive. Over and over in the air he turned, until he crashed against the water upside-down: a poor, ill-practiced dive, to be sure.

Then I swam a little away and turned to behold my work, resting upon the waves. Whenever the least stray part came near me, I struck it with my hind part so as to ensure these calves would not heal themselves. Then swiftly I drew back and came sideways, smiting the waters. Mouth below the water, I sang out a loud, short song and, as if they had been listening for just such a thing, the song of Whale came back.

It is he! It is he!
The lone one.

The only one.
The Last.

It is he.
The one who sings our fathers.
Their songs in his, his song in ours.
It is he who fights again.
And sings the battle's song.

Then I turned and made off, pushing my forehead through the ocean, dragging the wreckage of their carcasses and teeth behind me.

XXII. The Attack (Day III)

By the third day this battle upon the ocean had passed beyond Song and into the subtle noses and mouths of the waters, so that Shark arrived in a great host, following the dark Float Whale. Doubtless they had feasted on the little things and so marked their progenitor—not for itself but for its young and the things that fell from them and bled so abundantly.

The great surface-bound thing proved to me again its difference from the others of its kind when, Shark and all, it birthed its fanged young, and three calves moved toward me. Dived I did then and looked up to watch the slow, flailing younglings, while between us Shark in great number—teeth equally sharp—circled the oblivious calves.

Within me lay the thing that told me it was time—time to make full proof of what I was, even as I shared with my enemy the nature of what he was.

Tomorrow 'twill never be, the voice inside me said, *though we should live eternal.*

Then it lapsed into song: *Our time is all to-day, to-day. The same, though changed, and yet it flies.*

When it came time to draw breath, I propelled myself upward as I had the day previous, launching myself lengthwise from the waters. And as I did so I felt the Sea with me, as I had long ago in my youth. Upward she held me in the misty air, hovering longer than lay within my power alone, before I crashed back down into the deep. It was as if, for an instant, for some reason that was hers alone, she had cradled me in her grasp and then let me fall. Always she had known the degree of my care for her, but for the first time, I felt unconcealed the power of her care for me. A form of life and light she had taken on—a scene become part of sight. And in the instant she held me, she filled my being, just as I filled hers. And in my knowing she knew too and I saw for an instant all her vastness. And with it came a powerful new thing that I could not yet name. Indeed, so precious was she in that interval that all things one might desire failed in comparison.

The Sea was with me, as though we were one, and I wondered at how such a thing could be possible. But then I heard in all her music my own and recalled that which I thought I had never known: That nothing is impossible to a willing heart. And it was then I divined at last the nature of my enemy. That these killers were not hers, but rather monsters of Land come to make war upon her—upon me—and that the little things were as the hearts and minds of the Float Whale, and that one mind directed them all.

When I knew the Float Whale as the Sea did there arose in me another thing I had never before known. Wrath. Wrath at these little things—at their unnaturalness—but, mostly, wrath at the malice of the one directing mind, whose presence now I could feel. And so when I moved upon them, it was more furious even than before, smashing two of the dead calf things so that the Sea moved her waters open upon and over them. Yet, the third I left alone, for I knew it contained the mind that directed, and I felt its disfigured malice fixed upon me.

Then I turned and went, though without employing all my parts. I wished the dead calf thing to follow so that I might know which of the little things clinging to it thought and directed. Closer it came, closer still, and my eye strained among the little things to no avail. Closer it came, even alongside me, and it was then I discerned the ugly little thing. Rose it did, unsteadily, fang in hand and, with all its puny might, sunk its tooth into me. And with that bite—far worse than the bite—came the overwhelming malice of the little thing. So strong was it that I fairly threw it over.

In an instant I shot away from the dead calf thing and, turning suddenly in that manner I had learned long ago, snapping loose what held the hating thing's tooth. The float whale I once thought my great adversary, yet knew was but a dead hollow shell, lay before me, and upon it I directed new wrath, moving my parts to their limits, forehead parting the waters. The Sea swelled beneath me as I bore down so that all before me were as lost mad children at the hour when rock and ocean meet. When I struck the thing—which felt not like a whale at all, but rather blunted brittle coral—it stirred with a short uneasy motion. Then its front broke open like a clam and I saw that indeed it was but hollow and already dead, so that only the little things remained to be killed. A motley procession its brokenness made, with many a fleck of foam and fragment.

I took up a slow course, one I knew lay within the puny means of the remaining float thing to follow. And come it did, guided by the maliced one among them, who directed them all even as they moved alone upon the vast ocean. Closer I let them come, though not so close as before, for repugnant I found the little thing's hatred. Heaved the fang it did again and the tooth lodged firm, but thrash I did not. Instead I jerked my entire frame, leaping forward, and away came the little thing behind me, caught up in the ligaments of his own tooth, yet loosed from the safety of the mouth. Deep then I plunged, the malicious little thing winding about me and yet I felt its hate flowing from it with its life. And not just because it died, but because its search was over. It had found its thing at last—what's more, was with it—and from its tiny thought, growing ever smaller as death drew nigh, the hate fled entirely and for the thing's remaining instants, it was inhabited by a peace. Then I knew the Sea had taken it, but given before she took. Thus I minded not having it fastened to me like Barnacle or Bird. For they are things of the Sea and so then was it.

When at last I surfaced, the little thing long dead, but not without its gift from the Sea, I found the waters calm and all unnaturalness departed, save for one tiny dead float thing, which bore upon it a single one of the little things. I thought for a moment to bear down upon it, to erase this one smear from my beloved's otherwise perfect face—to allow no shadow of ravage, save that of the little thing's own. She was with me, but choice remained mine. And this gave me pause. I floated for a time, the Sea letting me watch the mind of the little thing. Gloomy, reticent, and secretive, it reckoned the Sea and I, but not without something akin to reverence. Mostly it was alone—despairingly alone—alone on the great, wide ocean. Slowly I moved away, resolving to give rather than take. And within me welled the pleasure of the Sea at my choice: to allow the little forsaken thing to go its way alone in the vast world, as I once had—a small thing myself—long ago.

Perhaps, my thought wandered further, this toothless little thing would live to tell the tale of what it saw. But first it must come to know the sweep of each sad lost wave. Then the waste, the far waste of waters and the soft lashing of the black waves—for long and in loneliness.

If it lay within this little one to learn such things, then perhaps there dwelt enough power within its puny frame to make a song. Of this I remained dubious, but I knew too that if these little things, however small they were, could exert from within them such terrible malice as the thing that had hated me, then might not they also prove capable of its opposite: the necessary thing for the greatest song and that which I now knew lay between the Sea and I, far mightier than either of us alone. Love.

XXIII. Epilogue

In the dark there was gentle floating somewhere between waking and sleep—consciousness trickling back into my brain as water slowly finds its way through rock. A strange variety of Bird cawed somewhere off in the distance. I felt a sandbar beneath me and the splashing of the waves.

Then a different sensation: something soft cleaning a raw place. Opening an eye, not without difficulty, I glimpsed an eye far smaller than mine: dark, untroubled, peering in curiosity with no apparent fear. As my gaze scrutinized the small orb, it widened then closed suddenly—a shy, young Whale calf cleaning my wound.

About us the unfamiliar harbor-bay was clear, calm, and tideless, and on it lay the shadow of Moon, who caused pale rock about me to shine bright. Steeped she was in stillness as she kept watch over me. The waters were calm, though the tide was full. Hollow murmurs died away and slumber took me again amid the bay's white, silent light.

Later, it was my maimed eye, so much the better, which opened to behold a gathering of calves wallowing inches from my head. And though I must have looked terrible to them, not a single one fled from my disfigurement, and in fact, seeing me awake, their soft tongues rose to clean about the raw, dried places cracked with salt.

When I gazed about me, I divined Whale as far as I could see against the early light and I knew this was a thing for me, just as—once, long ago—evening and morning had conspired to create the first day.

When my eyes were open, a song sprang among Whale which started close and spanned distant.

He lives! He lives!
The lone one.
The only one.
The Last.

He lives! He lives!
The one who sings our fathers.
Their songs in his, his song in ours
It is he who lives again
To sing again his songs.

A part of me wished to sing back to them, but my body had

emptied itself of words and too many other things. It was then I knew I had been lone too long alive in a world passed away: a place of phantoms, the dreams and fantasies of which a moment's achievement was destined to become tomorrow's confusion.

Slowly I began to rock back and forth, unmindful of my wounds, freeing myself at last from the sandbar when the tide swelled.

I turned seaward and as I did the various herds made way for me until naught but open water lay ahead.

Some of the larger of the bull calves moved out alongside me. Perhaps they wished to journey with me, which was not for them to do, or perhaps it was merely so that they could sing later of how they once had swum with me. Yet I heeded them not and kept my bearing straight, knowing to turn was to bleed away. I could not even feel my parts and yet on they bore me, as though I were the lightest of things.

Life is the preface to eternity, the Sea once had told me.

Slowly, as I moved onward, each young bull calf peeled away, until there was but one: a handsome fellow, less troubled by the distance. I knew he would be the one to lead them if he lived. But then he too was gone, returned to his kind. And I was left alone, as I always had been—a wild thing who had never saw fit to feel sorry for itself. Only this time it was not so much my own parts that guided me and I knew I was bound for a place in which everything I knew would be forgotten.

I did not sing, but listened instead to the sounds of the Sea. She had taken me back, just as she refuses no river, refuses no thing— however strange, lone, or wanton. The waters around me were gentle— calm, cloudless—and so I kept on a while, waiting for Moon to rise higher. And when she did, the old familiar glow on the water, I swiveled upon my back—teeth, blood, and all—to admire her in her fullness. Stiffness wracked all my parts, though not the vision of splendor. Indeed, it was if all the world were young, though I lay spent and old. Together they watched me, the Sea and her sister, and I felt within the Sea, as I had long ago, the thing she named Sadness. So I rose and dove: a deep, heavy dive—a good one. I might have settled for that as it was, but deeper I went and then deeper still, until the waters were dark—without dimension.

I found myself then arrived at a region. Yet even there, this nowhere, the Sea was still with me and, though I could discern no trace of her, so was Moon. And suddenly pinpoints of light appeared all about me in the blackness and I felt the gentle tug of Whirlpool, somewhere far beyond the place of Moon. I thought of a night long ago, recalling how every star was a Sun, each followed by his own herd of worlds.

I had arrived at a place I had never been—a place I knew lay beyond the power of all the world's oceans to follow. Yet it had opened for me and through untold vastness I moved, wan stars dancing between, and my parts gave back, even as they took, the light of ancient Suns. Dark it was and cold, but full of Song.

<u>Selected Poems Embedded in the Text</u>

A number of passages from *Moby Dick* are rephrased or employed outright in this narrative, as are single lines from numerous poems about the sea. What follows is a brief selection of those used at some length.

"The Ocean," Bjørnstjerne Bjørnson
"Nearer to Thee," Sarah Flower Evans
"The Poet and the Poem," Elizabeth Stuart Phelps
"Two Lovers and a Beachcomber By the Real Sea," Sylvia Plath

Casey Clabough is author or editor of over a dozen books. He splits his time between Cape Hatteras, North Carolina and Virginia